Copyright © 2015 by Randy Boyd.

All rights reserved. No part of this publication may be reproduced, distributed, or transmitted in any form or by any means, including photocopying, recording, or other electronic or mechanical methods, without the prior written permission of the publisher, except in the case of brief quotations embodied in critical reviews and certain other noncommercial uses permitted by copyright law. For permission requests, write to the publisher, addressed "Attention: Permissions Coordinator," at the address below:

Courageous Healers Publishing

P.O. Box 6506

La Quinta, CA

www.courageoushealers.org

Ordering Information:

Quantity sales: Special discounts are available on quantity purchases by corporations, associations, and others. For details, contact the "Special Sales Department" at the address above.

7-Day Challenge / Randy Boyd —1st edition

7-Day Challenge

"Whatever you can do or dream you can, begin it. Boldness has genius, power and magic in it!" ~Johann Wolfgang von Goethe

For most people in general, and almost all survivors, we spend all day every day surviving. This leads us to short term, quick fixes that tend to be detrimental in the long-term. It can often feel like the day is something we have to "get through," but setting aside a few minutes in which you deliberately search out your own peace and happiness can be the difference between surviving and thriving. The best news that I can give you is that a daily practice of gentle positive interaction with yourself will turn into a landslide of joy and healing.

Each of these seven challenges includes a journaling component. Journaling was probably the single most important tool during my early recovery and is a daily activity included as a component of each of the 7-day challenges. I suggest you journal first thing in the morning, and before you go to bed at night. For me, it was a way to safely express the feelings and emotions that I had locked away when I was growing up. Something wonderful happens during journaling. Problems resolve themselves, issues clear up, and things I have been stressing out over shrink down to their proper size.

For this challenge, I encourage you to try it for yourself. Pick up a notepad – one that you can keep with you as you go about your day. It is the best friend you could have during those moments of stress and frustration where you might otherwise say or do something you regret – like numb out with drugs or alcohol, or snap at your spouse, boss, or children. You can say whatever you want in a journal and you won't hurt anyone. You have at your fingertips the most patient, trustworthy friend in the world. Sometimes we just need to vomit all the vile thoughts and rage inside of us, and journaling gives us a friend who is always ready to listen. During the next seven days as you walk on this journey, take an extra minute or two each day to jot down your experiences. You can release your stressful feelings, your hurt and your anger through journaling and celebrate your victories and accomplishments.

Here's to an amazing seven-day challenge. Give each of these practices a try and see which ones you gravitate towards. Treat your healing like an experiment; try not to prejudge suggestions until you have actually tried them out for yourself. Most importantly, be kind and gentle with yourself. If you forget or don't complete a day, it's okay. Just get up the next day and start again.

When it comes to healing yourself and learning to be happy, you can't do it wrong. Even if you give up completely, you will eventually come back to a place where you are tired of feeling miserable and ready to try something new. You cannot do this wrong. So have a little fun – abuse has stolen enough time from you – today is the day you stand up and say, no more. Today is the day that just surviving is no longer good enough. Today, you, my fellow survivor, get to start to thrive.

Day 1: Mindfulness (Two 10-minute sessions)

> "Half an hour's meditation each day is essential, except when you are busy. Then a full hour is needed." ~St. Francis de Sales

Note: I strongly suggest that you make a daily habit of some type of mindful meditation. Here it is listed as the activity for Day One, but if you add these ten-minute sessions into the next seven days it will greatly improve your results for every other practice.

We have what psychologists call automatic cognitive biases, which, if unchecked, run us through the ringer every day. These biases can trigger habitual negative thoughts like, "the world isn't safe," or "no one loves me," or "I'm not good enough." As information pours in via our senses, we make assumptions every second based on those cognitive biases.

> "Everyone creates realities based on their own personal beliefs. These beliefs are so powerful that they can create [expansive or entrapping] realities over and over. ~Kuan Yin"

As you can imagine, the cognitive biases for survivors aren't pretty. They turn our lives into mine fields with painful experiences erupting out of perfectly harmless moments. In Chapter 3 we discuss triggers, which are sensory inputs that can trigger a memory or flashback to a previous experience. Survivors tend to be hair-triggered to past pain and sometimes going through the day can feel like we are frogs reeling from one hot rock to another.

Strengthening metacognitive control in order to overcome cognitive biases is a fancy way of saying that we learn how to stop and think before we erupt into a painful reaction. We need to learn how to get some leverage on our emotional triggers. Practicing mindfulness is, in my opinion (which is shared by some of our leading neuroscientists these days), the simplest, most natural way to give ourselves a break.

SESSION ONE:
WALKING MINDFULNESS
(10 MINUTES)

Take yourself on a walk today. As you walk, look around and just notice the sights and smells and sensations. Give everything you see a one-word, non-qualitative name. For example, walking down the street, my inner naming dialogue might sound like, "street, grass, tree, sky, car, human, ball, dog, bike, sign, cloud, bee, ant, park..." etc. Don't apply any judgment to what you see and avoid all adjectives. Simply walk and list what you see.

It doesn't matter what you name the things you see. You can call a car a balloon if you want. The idea is to simply move through the world without judging the things around you, learning to observe and be present.

You can take this practice with you throughout your day. If you feel yourself starting to become agitated or stressed, just take a trip to the bathroom and walk down the hallway, returning to this walking meditation.

After your walk, take a few minutes to journal about your experience. Remember, in journaling, don't self-edit. The objective is to keep your pencil moving for a given period of time. Set a timer for five minutes and write the whole time. It's okay if you literally write, "I don't know what to write," over and over again. Eventually other words will come. Have fun with this. See how long you can keep the pencil moving.

My experience with walking mindfulness:

SESSION TWO:
SITTING MEDITATION (10 MINUTES)

There are many, many books and seminars to teach you all the different ways to meditate. I am going to give you the one that has impacted me the most positively in the least amount of time – given me the best "bang for my buck," so to speak.

Find a quiet spot. It doesn't matter where it is. The only thing that matters is that you won't be interrupted for at least ten minutes. I have found that bathrooms make great meditation rooms, as do cars and even dressing rooms in a pinch. I don't like the idea of creating a formal "meditation room," when you begin because it makes it seem like meditation is only something that can only be done in a special room at a special time.

The best way to use this tool is to spread it all over your life. Sure, it's great to sit down in a beautiful space with candles and pictures and music. But sometimes I most need to meditate when I am in the middle of traffic or just after I get off of a phone call that left my shoulders locked up around my ears. Meditation is not a special, mystical thing – it's a natural state of intentional relaxation and positivity. Any spot that is quiet and will give you at least ten minutes of uninterrupted time is perfect.

Sit comfortably. It's hard to "be natural" on purpose – you are looking for a state of relaxed alertness. One important thing that I learned the hard way is that meditation time is not naptime. You won't get the benefits of meditation if you fall asleep, so find a physical position that helps you stay relaxed, but alert. *If you are sleepy, I suggest walking meditation instead so that you don't lose out on your meditation time by falling asleep.*

You can close your eyes or leave them open. I tend to close them for sitting meditations. Start by finding your breath. Notice where it comes into your body, how it fills your lungs and raises your chest, and how it feels when you exhale. Your breath is your anchor, your ground, your "home base."

If you get lost in a memory of the past or a projection into the future, bring yourself back to home base. You have 23 hours and fifty minutes today in which you can project into the future and dig around in the past. These are ten special minutes in which you can just be yourself, relaxed, peaceful and comfortable.

As you sit and notice your breath, remind yourself that you are here to train your mind. Our minds are like ADHD squirrels. Taming that squirrel will take some practice. The way we do it is just by noticing when the squirrel starts to dart off towards the future or the past.

When we find ourselves running off into a story, just name the story, like you did in your walking meditation, and come back to the breath. Your squirrel mind will try to convince you that whatever it starts thinking about is much more important than meditation. But remind it kindly but firmly, that everything can wait for a few minutes and gently return to noticing your breath.

Take a minute or two before you start and after you finish to journal your experience.

My experience before meditation:

_____
_____
_____
_____
_____
_____

My experience after meditation:

Day Two: Your Gratitude and Victory Journal
(5 minutes)

"Gratitude is the ability to experience life as a gift. It liberates us from the prison of self-preoccupation." ~John Ortberg, When the Game Is Over, It All Goes Back in the Box

Unless someone has experienced chronic emotional pain from trauma or abuse, they don't really know what survivors face on a daily basis. Some days, it seems so bleak that we can't even imagine ever climbing out of the hole we are in. Depression, rage, shame, anger, frustration and fear become our way of life until we consciously work to change it.

One of the easiest ways to do this is to keep a gratitude and victory journal. I keep mine by my bedside. When I wake in the morning and before I fall asleep at night, I write down at least three things I am grateful for and three things that I considered victories in that day.

Sometimes it feels good to write for a few pages, either listing more things that I am grateful for or writing down additional victories, or expanding on a few. Sometimes there are just six short words scrawled in my journal. But no matter what, I make sure that sometime during the day I have trained my mind to focus on at least three victories and three things I am grateful for.

Even without a history of trauma and abuse, the human mind is conditioned to think negatively, and with a history of trauma and abuse, one negative thought can quickly spiral down into shame attack or depression.

The gratitude and victory journal is a simple, easy, quick way to train our minds out of its habitual negativity. The abuse has stolen enough of our happiness. This journal is one way to start reclaiming it.

I am going to suggest that you journal by hand. When you use a pen or pencil and paper, something magical happens between your head, heart, hand, and the paper, which can only be experienced not explained. It is too easy to stop and edit your writing on a computer. The idea when journaling is to put your pen/pencil on the paper and just write without stopping

The process is simple and easy. Every day, write down three things that you are grateful for *that day* and three things that you consider victories. Here is a sample from my own journal:

> 7:00 p.m. October 15, 2014
>
> Gratitude: I am grateful for the ability to be able to express my self freely in this journal, I am grateful for my dogs that always show me unconditional love and most importantly I am grateful for my loving and gracious God.
>
> Victories: Today I was able to support my wife effectively when she went to get her MRI. This time I didn't try to talk to her or reason with her panic. I just sat next to her, holding her hand and being quiet and supportive. I don't know if it was because of the change in my behavior, but she didn't have a panic attack (I'm also grateful for that!), and this time we both left the doctor's office much less stressed out!
>
> Victories: On my bike ride today, I beat my bets time from my house to the top of the cove by 15 seconds.
>
> Victories: I conquered my fear of doing a guitar recital in front of y maestro.
>
> Today I am grateful that I for the soldiers that fight for our freedom, the freedom theta allows me to sleep peacefully in my bed, next to my wife, while that same soldier is sleeping in a foxhole in the middle of a war ravaged desert.
>
> Today I am grateful I did not need to drink alcohol or use a drug.

My journal entries vary greatly. Some days are great and I have all the time and energy to write a few pages. Other days it's a stretch to find even one thing that I felt grateful for or that I could count as a victory.

> 8:45p.m. November 11, 2015

> *Gratitude: I'm grateful for dinner. I'm grateful that my bird loves me best. I'm grateful for my toothbrush.*
>
> *Victories: I brushed my teeth twice today. I took the trash out. I did my math homework.*

If that last entry sounds a bit like a sullen teenager, that's because I was feeling like a sullen teenager. It doesn't matter that I had a bad day. What matters is that I took the time to do the gratitude and victory journal anyway. It's important to make this a habit every day, but especially on the bad days.

The bad days are where the smallest efforts return the biggest rewards. Teaching myself how to find positivity even when I feel horrible has paid off in huge returns in my life. I notice that, as a result of this practice, I am no longer able to sink as deeply into self-pity or despair.

> *"I'm thankful for a pair of shoes that feel really good on my feet; I like my shoes."*
>
> *I'm thankful for the birds; I feel like they're singing just for me when I get up in the morning... Saying, 'Good morning, John. You made it, John.'*
>
> *I'm thankful for the sea breeze that feels so good right now, and the scent of jasmine when the sun starts going down.*
>
> *I'm thankful..."* ~Johnny Cash

Looking for the positive, for things to be grateful for, and even the small victories has made me mentally tougher and more resilient, less pessimistic and more empowered. Give it a shot. It just might be the most important three minutes of your day.

As before, I encourage you to take a few moments to jot down how you are feeling before, and then how you feel after as a part of this exercise. There are no "right" answers. The point of this journaling is not to be able to say, "I felt bad before and good afterwards," but to get into the habit of noticing your emotions and developing the practice of writing them down. My experience is that negative emotions become smaller, less profound and positive emotions grow in power when I write them down, but this is your seven-day challenge and your experience in journaling. Remember to treat each new process like an experiment, see what works for you and what doesn't. Journaling is not only part of that discovery, it is an additional "bonus" process.

Before doing my gratitude and victory journal, I feel my day and emotional state was:

_____
_____
_____
_____
_____
_____

After doing my gratitude and victory journal I feel my day and emotion state is:

_____
_____
_____
_____
_____
_____
_____
_____

Three things I am grateful for:

1.)
___

2.)
___

3.)
___

My three victories today were:

1.)

2.)

3.)

Day Three: Laughter and Smile Therapy

"Smile, it's free therapy." ~Douglas Horton

Laughter really is the best medicine. Studies show that people who laugh and smile more are happier. Sounds obvious, right? But it turns out it's not just that people who are happy tend to smile more... researchers are discovering that that just the physical act of smiling can make you happier.

According to psychologist Paul Ekman, laughing and smiling cause the brain to release the "feel-good" hormone dopamine. Experts all over the scientific community are finding that smiling and laughing have emotional, mental, and even physiological health benefits. It's free, it's easy, and it's fast. Even faking a smile causes your brain to release these feel-good chemicals. Smile therapy is easy.

Step 1: Take an ordinary pencil or pen and put it in your mouth, then bite down on it horizontally. Step 2: Smile. Step 3: Continue for at least five minutes. Step 4: Enjoy the feel-good chemicals that flood your brain automatically. There is one caveat...while you technically *could* do it anywhere, I don't necessarily recommend it. It can look a little strange if you don't let people know what's going on!

While smile therapy works even if the smile isn't genuine, I find that it's more fun to find things that make you smile or laugh. There are funny animal and prank videos all over the Internet and if I can't find something online, stand-up comedy always does the trick for me.

Often time while driving down the highway or just walking and talking with my wife about life, she will glance at me and seeing that I am agitated, she says to me – *Give me a one-minute smile!* At first I am resistant, yet she persist with her goofy one-minute smile, and before I know it I am laughing uncontrollably – instantly my attitude changes from angry to happy. Give it a try, what do you have to loose?

"Laughter is carbonated holiness." ~Anne Lamott

Whether or not you search out something that leaves you laughing hysterically, or you simply paste on a smile even though it's the last thing you feel like doing, today's challenge is to smile (or laugh) for five minutes twice today.

Jot down a quick entry about how you felt before each five-minute session and how you felt after.

Session 1
Before laughing:
_____
_____
_____
_____

After laughing:
_____
_____
_____
_____

Session 2
Before laughing:
_____
_____
_____
_____

After laughing:

_____
_____
_____
_____

Day Four: Getting to Know Your Inner Child

"Caring for your inner child has a powerful and surprisingly quick result: Do it and the child heals." ~Martha Beck

Chapter 2 focuses on the idea that, even though we cannot literally go back and recreate the ideal childhood, we can, starting now, create a happy childhood for the hurt, angry and scared inner child inside of us. If this sounds a bit hokey to you, believe me, I know how you feel. I felt the same way. But I simply cannot argue with the results.

Learning how to re-parent my inner child has been the single most powerful healing tool I have ever found. If you are serious about wanting to heal from the pain of your past, I hope that you will trust my experience enough to try this out.

In every real man a child is hidden that wants to play.
~Friedrich Nietzsche

While everyone can benefit from inner child work, survivors have the most to gain. Childhood abuse often leaves the survivor "stuck" at the age the abuse began. This inner child is often scared and hurting.

"A grownup is a child with layers on." ~Woody Harrelson

When starting the dialogue with your inner child, it's important to remember that you will be dealing with a child. A hurt and traumatized one, so it's even more important to be your best self when interacting with him (or her). The first step is willingness. You have to be willing to meet your inner child; you have to genuinely want to know him. If you aren't sincere, wait to start this process until you can be totally committed.

When you are ready, be prepared to ask a lot of questions. When you first "meet" your inner child, you might not know what to say or do. That's okay! Just ask questions the way you would if you were meeting an actual child for the first time.

Here are some suggested questions for that first meeting:

Hi! What's your name?

How old are you?

What's your favorite color?

What do you like to do?

How do you feel today?

Are you happy/mad/angry/scared/lonely/sad?

Do you want to play?

What do you need?

What's your favorite thing to do?

What do you want to be when you grow up?

Do you know that I love you?

You can ask these questions any way that works best for you. Some people have the best results just sitting quietly and asking and waiting for an auditory answer. That didn't really work for me.

My best results were from journaling, and then later, from non-dominant hand journaling. If you choose journaling, remember that children are direct. They can communicate in just a few words. At other times, they may ramble, and want patience to express themselves.

> *"Our inner child is still in there somewhere, aching to be let loose from all the layers we've piled on over the years. Why not break him or her out for the day or even a moment?"* ~Lynn Hasselberger

One exercise that I have found to be very effective for "first time" meetings is a combination of dominant and non-dominant journaling. To try this method, take two pencils. With your dominant hand ask questions from your adult self. Let your child answer through your non-dominant hand.

The most important thing is to suspend judgment. Just the answers arise naturally; don't judge the answers, don't edit them. Some of the responses might surprise or even shock you. Some of the answers might even hurt you, or make you angry. Remember that the part of you that is talking is a wounded child. Treat yourself the same way you would treat an abused child. In order to heal, we must learn to love and accept ourselves.

Many survivors find it much easier to love and accept their inner child because they understand that the child inside is hurting badly. The natural response to a wounded child is to provide loving, non-judgmental comfort. In learning how to do this for our inner child, we learn how to do it for our adult self as well.

I have experienced the gamut of responses from my own inner child, as well as helping other survivors through the process. Your inner child might be ecstatic to hear from you and ready to talk right away. Or he might be sullen and pout for a while before he is ready to answer your questions. Just be patient and make sure that he knows that he is safe, cared for, and worth your time. Let him know that you are willing to take as long as he needs because you love him.

If you are having trouble being patient and loving, make sure you communicate honestly and fairly. Just imagine the way you wish your parents had communicated with you when you were a child.

For example, if you have a strong reaction to something that your inner child says, instead of shutting down, getting angry or going away, communicate those emotions. Try saying, *I'm having a hard time processing what you just said because I feel sad/mad/scared/hurt/ashamed. I want you to know that I am not upset with you. I just need a little time to process my own emotions. I am going to go and work on this by myself for a little while. I promise to come back and talk with you about it in a hour/tomorrow/next week/in the morning/etc.*

It is important that you give your child a promise to come back... and it is incredibly important that you keep that promise. As adults we want to be able to trust others to hear us out, to love us no matter what we say, and to keep their promises to us.

Children are the same. In order to build trust, it is crucial that you keep your promises, communicate openly and stay gentle and loving. Give yourself a whole heaping pile of credit for every attempt you make, for every promise you keep and for every time you provide the loving space that you didn't get when you were a child.

As always, take a few extra minutes before and after today's challenge to jot down some notes about your experience.

Randy's opening dialogue with his inner child:

4/27/09 God ①

adult: I don't like being alone
child: Wheather do I
Adult: Whats your name?
Child: It's Randy silly You know my name
adult: Yes, I just wanted to make sure, because as confused as I am yet, I can imagine how confused you must be.
Child: actually I'm not that confused
adult: your not?
Child: No
adult: then how come I am?
child: I don't know, maybe because your an adult now
adult: how old are you?
child: 5
adult: are you sure? you seemed a bit confused when you answered.
Child: there you go again doubting me to make me do what you want. Maybe so, I'm 5 years old.
adult: ok your right. I'm sorry. Hey I have to go now to my meeting. But I'll be back.

23

Opening dialogue with my inner child:

My dialogue with my inner child
If you get stuck, refer to the questions on page 20 to help you get started.

Before journaling with my inner child I my day emotional state was:

_____
_____
_____
_____
_____
_____
_____
_____
_____
_____
_____
_____
_____
_____
_____
_____
_____
_____
_____
_____
_____
_____
_____
_____
_____
_____
_____
_____
_____
_____

After journaling with my inner child I my day emotional state is:

Day Five: Secret Random Acts of Kindness

"That best portion of a man's life, his little, nameless, unremembered acts of kindness and love." ~William Wordsworth

I've been on this journey for a while now. Most of the time I feel pretty good – better than I've ever felt, actually. I feel positive and optimistic, I like myself, and I am able to trust the world and the people in it. I feel connected to God, to nature, to my friends, my family and to myself.

And then there are the bad days. Days when I feel the old shame cycle start up again. On those days, all it takes is one wrong word or look to trigger me and send me into a spiral of anger or depression. Days when the old feeling that the world would be better off without me comes back and sucker punches me right in the gut.

Those days will come, but I've found a good way to keep them from dragging me all the way down to despair and suicidal ideation. I practice secret acts of kindness. I got the idea from a friend who had been to Byron Katie's 9-day School for the Work – an incredible retreat where you work to undo your own stressful thoughts. At that retreat, Katie suggests to the participants that everyday, each person commits three secret acts of kindness *without getting caught.*

I don't know what Katie's reasoning is, but as far as how a survivor's mind works, this is brilliant. Because, for a variety of reasons, the vast majority of us missed out on the chance to bond with our primary caregivers, we go through life desperately seeking validation and approval from others. The problem is that we forget how to approve of ourselves.

We become dependent on other people's approval and we start to become emotional chameleons, twisting ourselves into whatever we think will be most likely to make someone else like us, usually at our own expense.

We say yes when we mean no, we do things we don't want to do, say things we don't mean, and let ourselves down time and time again just so that we can fill our approval cup. But what we don't realize is that every approval cup has a whole in the bottom.

Approval drains out as fast as it comes in and enough is never enough. The only kind of approval that can really fill us up is our own. And when we are constantly seeking approval from other people, we cannot approve of ourselves. You know that feeling you get inside when you say yes to someone when you really want to say no?

It's this sickening feeling in the pit of the stomach that just makes you disgusted with yourself for a split second. Of course we don't approve of ourselves. We know that we are lying, needy, and being manipulative...we might be able to fool the other person into approving of us, but it *comes at the expense of our own approval*. And that is too high a price to pay.

So this exercise reverses that cycle. Instead of doing things to garner admiration or approval from other people, we do it 100% for our own approval. And, I have to tell you it feels amazing. Not only does it just plain feel good to secretly do nice things for other people, it completely destroys the power of the all-too-familiar "the world would be better off without you," thought.

"The smallest act of kindness is worth more than the grandest intention." ~ Oscar Wilde

There are no rules for this exercise other than "don't get caught." You might clean up a public restroom, leave a nice note someplace, pay for the coffee of the person behind you in line, leave a flower on someone's windshield...the possibilities are endless. Have fun, be creative and don't get caught!

My experience-practicing secret random acts of kindness:

Day Six: Artistic Expression - Finding an Outlet in the Arts

> *"Art washes away from the soul the dust of every day life."* ~ Pablo Picasso

You don't have to be DaVinci or Mozart to get the benefits of art and music. Self-expression through the arts is a type of emotional shorthand. It allows you to go directly from experience to expression without the difficulty that some of us have when it comes to putting feelings into words.

Even in the twenty-first century, western gender roles still tell men that we aren't supposed to have feelings, let alone talk about them. I play the guitar and draw. I'm never going to play at Carnegie Hall and my drawings are never going to go up on the walls of an art exhibit... but that's not the point. Playing my guitar focuses my mind, not only on the present, which offers great benefits to mindfulness, but on the creation of something beautiful. Playing the guitar improves my self-esteem, calms me down, makes me happy and reduces my stress. Likewise with art... although, I had to get past the idea that I "couldn't draw," and "wasn't artistically talented." The only way to ruin this healing technique is to start thinking about what other people would think about your art, music or dancing.

Your job for this challenge is to stop caring what anyone thinks, lock yourself away and paint, draw, dance, sing or play an instrument like you did when you were a kid. No one is ever going to see, hear or watch you... this is only for you. You can turn on your favorite mix and just boogie down by yourself for fifteen minutes, you can grab a hairbrush and sing along, or you can go to the art supply store or music store and investigate a more long-term investment into this healing therapy.

If you've ever thought about playing the drums, or picking up the clarinet again, this is your chance. If you've secretly had a hankering to splatter some paint on a canvas, now's the time. Life is short and you've wasted enough time worrying about what other people will think. Remember, the entire recovery journey does not have to be talk-therapy, tears and deep revelations. Expressing yourself creatively is equally important. So get out there and have some fun!

After you're done, take another five minutes to jot down your experience.

I promise myself that today I will:
- *Sing*
- *Dance*
- *Draw/Paint/Sculpt*
- *Play a musical instrument*

For a minimum of 20 minutes

Name:_____ Signature:_____

My experience with being creative:

_____
_____
_____
_____
_____
_____
_____
_____
_____
_____
_____

Day Seven: Get Happy

> *"True happiness...arises, in the first place, from the enjoyment of one's self."*
> ~Joseph Addison

Why is it that we are so good at making ourselves miserable but we are lost when it comes to actively cultivating our own happiness? I don't mean the momentary happiness that comes from purchasing something new, winning an argument or receiving a compliment... I mean the deep, intrinsic, spiritual happiness that comes from inside of us. In Chapter 7 we talk about living from your authentic self and following your bliss - words that are easy to say but surprisingly difficult to do.

In today's high-tech, fast-paced society it's easy to forget that the whole point of the car, the job, the education, the vacations, the family time, is to...be happy. We think that if we can just land this promotion, or marry this girl, or buy this house, then, finally, we will be happy. But if you've lived long enough, you know that it doesn't work like that.

Happiness is found in the in-between moments in life. The times when you stop being busy for one moment, happiness sometimes sneaks up and hits you right between the eyes. I used to feel like depression and despair were constantly surrounding me, just waiting for my guard to drop so that they could finally surround me and take me over. I stayed busy, even while I was ostensibly having fun, all the time as a defense against that constant fear. What I discovered when I finally found the courage to stop, take a deep breath and face those demons shocked me.

Happiness was waiting for me. It isn't sadness and despair that we have been barricading ourselves against for so long...happiness waits for us in the small moments between one thought and the next, in the space between one action and the next. Today's challenge is about re-learning how to be a happy human being instead of a stressed-out human-doing.

I've found that being good at being happy is just like anything else – to be good at anything, you've got to practice. Practicing being happy, for me, comes in two parts. One is a focused type of happy-meditation. The other is in recognizing happy moments in my day-to-day life and "milking them" for all they're worth.

> *"The foolish man seeks happiness in the distance, the wise grows it under his feet."*
> *~James Oppenheim*

Let's start with the first practice. Find a quiet spot and sit quietly, just like we did on the first day of our challenge, start to focus on your breath. Now find something that you're grateful for, without any strings attached.

Pure, positive, unadulterated gratitude is a lot like happiness. But it has to be clean. Anything with strings attached won't work. For example, it doesn't work to say, "I'm grateful that my boss wasn't a complete moron today," or "I'm grateful that today I didn't want to die." Those are backwards thoughts and have a heavy feeling to them. It might take a while to find something for which you are wholly, purely, cleanly grateful, or which makes you happy.

When I struggle to find one, I have my "go-to" thoughts. I think of the way my dog, Tucker, greets me when I get home after being away for a few days, or the feeling I get at the end of a long bike ride, and the wind is cool in my hair and my muscles are tired but alive.

Find something, (it can be anything at all, big or small) which rings true for you and lifts your heart. Now breathe into that feeling, deliberately expanding it and letting it fill your chest. With each new breath, imagine that feeling spreading through your body, and the space in your chest getting bigger and bigger. Continue to breathe into this feeling of love and gratitude for as long as you can. When you feel it start to fade, ask yourself to find a new happy thought and then breathe into that new thought. Do this for five minutes.

For the other five minutes of today's challenge, stay present with yourself as you go throughout the day and notice the things you see that make you happy. A poster on the street, a boy walking his dog, the sky, the smile of a cashier, a song on the radio, a post on the internet or a funny video.

Notice these tiny moments and repeat the exercise from this morning. Breathe into the moment, deliberately expanding the spark of happiness.

And, as always, take a few moments to jot down your experiences.

My experience before deliberately cultivating happiness today:

_____
_____
_____
_____
_____
_____
_____
_____

My experience before:

Closing Thoughts

These seven days can be a jumpstart into a new way of being, if you let them. We have been beaten down, lost in a haze of pain and shame for too long. It's time to pick ourselves up and decide that we deserve to be happy, we deserve to heal, and we deserve to have a wonderful rest of our life.

Many of us have spent decades learning how to be miserable, we know how to be mistrustful, how to be angry and defensive, quick to despair or to attack. And even though those coping skills may have gotten us to this point, they have not made us happy.

It's time to try a new way of being in the world. Sexual abuse doesn't have to be a life sentence of pain and loneliness. We can, with practice, turn that pain into strength and the sadness into joy. I know this is true because I have done it, and I have walked with hundreds of other survivors through the same processes out of the darkness.

Here's to your healing and your happiness. If you would like to stay in touch, my blog is at *www.courageoushealers.org*. I look forward to hearing about your journey!

Websites

www.courageoushealers.org

www.changeyourlifestorynow.com

www.thehealingman.wordpress.com

www.malesurvivor.org

www.1in6.org

For our annual "It Happens to Boys" conferences go to: www.creativechangeconferences.com

For the Gender Matters, Men Matter conference go to: www.CedarColorado.org

ABOUT THE AUTHOR

Randy Boyd, founder of the Courageous Healers Foundation, has been working with male survivors of sexual abuse to help transform their pain into joy and their shame into strength. Sober since 2007, Randy has rededicated his life to helping male survivors regain their sense of self-worth. Every year, Randy speaks at dozens of conferences, schools, treatment facilities, and homes about the effects of sexual abuse on men, and how to start healing the wounds. A licensed California Alcohol and Drug Counselor and Certified Life Coach, Randy is currently pursuing a degree in psychology. Randy currently lives in the Coachella Valley with his wife of thirty

www.ingramcontent.com/pod-product-compliance
Lightning Source LLC
Chambersburg PA
CBHW031508040426
42444CB00007B/1252